I0088034

Beyond the Prompt

Leading with Purpose in the Age of AI

JOE CURCILLO

The Generalist's Advantage Leadership Series

Beyond the Prompt: Leading with Purpose in the Age of AI
by Joe Curcillo

For information, contact:
Synergy Thinkers Press

**Synergy
Thinkers
Press**

Harrisburg, Pennsylvania
www.TheGeneralistsAdvantage.com

ISBN: 978-1-7324856-4-8 (paperback)

First Edition

Printed in the United States of America

Any sufficiently advanced technology is indistinguishable from magic.

— *Arthur C. Clarke, Clarke's Third Law*

Table of Contents

Executive Guide
How to Use This Book

Beyond the Prompt isn't a manual for mastering AI. It's a leadership field guide for CEOs, executives, and strategic decision-makers who navigate systems accelerated by AI.

This book isn't about chasing the next tool. It's about leading across complexity with judgment, humanity, and systems thinking.

Use it this way:

- Read Part I ("The New Terrain") to reframe leadership in the AI era.

- Apply Part II ("The Generalist Edge") to lead beyond technology, through systems, people, and long-view consequences.

- Reference the Appendices for ethical checks, reflection prompts, and leadership tools built for boardrooms and strategic pivots.

This isn't a book to skim and shelve.
It's a resource to reach for when clarity matters most.

When the noise gets loud, when the pace accelerates, when the stakes get real—use this book to lead like it still matters.

Because it does. Now more than ever.

This Isn't About Panic

You don't need to master every algorithm. You need to stay grounded and lead with clarity.

WHEN AI BECAME publicly available in November 2022, I dove in—not just out of curiosity, but because I wanted to understand what was really happening under the surface. I've spent years since then working with executives and leadership teams, studying not just the tools themselves but the larger system they're reshaping.

What fascinated me wasn't just the technology. It was how quickly a wave of so-called "experts" emerged—people who could write clever prompts, build flashy tools, and surf the latest trends, but who didn't truly understand the deeper forces they were playing with. AI isn't static. It evolves by the day. Mastery isn't about tricks; it's about seeing the system, the consequences, and the patterns unfolding underneath.

Along the way, I saw something else—something more concerning. Even the most capable leaders I knew, the ones who had navigated every wave of change before, were starting to feel a quiet intimidation. They weren't afraid of the technology itself. They were overwhelmed by the noise. The hype. The sense that somehow, without warning, the ground rules had changed.

That's why I wrote this book.

Not to predict the future. Not to join the chorus of hype. But to quiet the panic—and to give serious leaders a different lens. AI is not something to fear. It's something to understand and to lead through with clarity, judgment, and courage.

The world is moving faster. The tools are getting smarter. But leadership—the real kind—has never been more important. This moment isn't about becoming a technical expert. It's about sharpening your instincts, strengthening your systems view, and guiding your teams through complexities that technology alone can't solve.

This book is for the generalists—the leaders who see across lanes, connect what others separate, and hold steady when others rush. It's for the people you lead, those who look to you for direction, discernment, and human judgment when the systems around them accelerate beyond recognition.

You don't have to chase every trend.

You just have to remember who you are—and lead from there.

Because beyond the prompt is where leadership lives.

Why We Still Need a Human Touch

AI IS GETTING better. Fast.

It can write, summarize, predict, automate, and optimize almost every domain of work. The tools are fundamental, the impact is real, and the shift we're experiencing isn't minor.

Leadership still requires a human. Not because machines are broken. But because they weren't built to hold what we hold.

Leadership still requires a human. Not because machines are broken. But because they weren't built to hold what we hold.

But here's what hasn't changed:

Leadership still requires a human.

Not because machines are broken. But because they weren't built to hold what we hold.

AI doesn't understand the consequences.

It doesn't recognize trade-offs.

It can't weigh context, culture, or timing.

And it doesn't carry the weight of a decision once it's made. That's still on us.

To lead now is to go beyond the prompt—to take what the system gives you and ask: "What does this actually mean? Who does it affect? Where does it land in the real world?"

Because leadership isn't in the draft. It's in the decision.

In 2024, McKinsey & Company reported that while over 65% of organizations were regularly using generative AI in at least one business function, leaders were not simply accepting outputs at face value. Instead, they were actively reshaping them—refining AI-generated ideas to align with their company's strategic vision, brand voice, and human nuance.[1] "It's useless," they said. "Generic. Empty. It doesn't sound like us at all."

And they were right—partially.

The output wasn't wrong.

It just wasn't finished.

Even though generative AI can quickly produce a plan or design, it lacks the contextual judgment to make trade-offs or weigh consequences. Human oversight is still crucial.

AI had handed them the structure—the scaffolding, the raw material. But it couldn't give them the human touch-points, the strategic nuance, the lived reality of what the company stood for. That part was still theirs to bring.

---

[1] McKinsey & Company, "How AI is Transforming Strategy Development," March 2024. https://www.mckinsey.com/capabilities/strategy-and-corporate-finance/our-insights/how-ai-is-transforming-strategy-development

They didn't recognize that leadership isn't in getting a perfect draft from a machine. It's in shaping it—infusing it with the judgment, context, and meaning that no system can replicate.

AI can give you the outline. But it's still on you to go beyond the prompt—to bring vision, consequence, and meaning no machine can replicate. This book helps you lead beyond the prompt—past the quick answers, and toward the deeper questions that shape the future. That's human leadership.

And that's the part you can't automate.

That's what generalists do.

We don't just look at the result—we scan the ripple. We don't just ask if the solution works—we ask for whom, when, and at what cost.

If you've lived in multiple lanes, led across differences, or found yourself making calls without a clear precedent, you already know what this moment feels like. The pace is fast. The pressure is high. And more often than not, the map doesn't match the terrain.

This book isn't about resisting the future. It's about showing up for it.

It's here to help generalist leaders stay calm, clear, and steady as the systems around them accelerate. It's here to help you guide your teams—not just in what to do, but in how to think about what we're building and who it's for.

This book is here to help you do that.

Not to outpace the machine—but to lead past it.

To stay human. Stay present. Stay purposeful.

To lead beyond the prompt.

PART I

THE NEW TERRAIN

In a world flooded with faster answers,
the edge belongs to those who can connect,
contextualize, and lead beyond the noise.

Chapter 1

What AI Can Do— and What It Can't

NOW THAT WE understand why human judgment remains essential, let's explore precisely what the landscape looks like. We'll first get clear about exactly what AI does well—and, more importantly, what it can't replace.

Let's clear something up right away: I'm not here to knock on the machine.

AI is fast. It's scalable. It's great at patterns—better than you, better than me. It can scrape every database in the world before your coffee cools. It can generate twenty options while you're still thinking about the question.

Yes, it wins with speed, precision, and brute-force analysis—in those areas, it's a game-changer. But when it comes to leadership, it fails.

Leadership is about people.

It isn't a data problem.

And that's where the machine runs out of road.

Because AI can't sit in the fog and hold tension, it can't read the emotional temperature of a room teetering on the edge. It can't feel the weight of a decision or recognize when the obvious answer is wrong. Not because it's broken, but because it was never built for that.

It doesn't have a conscience. It doesn't have context. It doesn't carry consequences.

We do.

What the Machine Does Well

Let's give AI its due.

- Speed: Need a hundred options? Need them now? It's already done.
- Scale: It can process more data in seconds than you'll see in a lifetime.
- Pattern Recognition: It's the world's best pattern matcher—across language, images, diagnostics, you name it.

If you're making a purely logical, bounded, and well-defined decision, AI can crush it.

But most leadership decisions? They're the opposite of that.

They're messy.

They're emotional.

They involve people, politics, perception, and trade-offs you can't automate away.

Technology moves fast—but direction still demands human hands.

What It Can't Do (And Why That Matters)

Here's what the machine can't do—and what makes generalist leaders more essential than ever.

1. **It can't hold ambiguity.**

   AI needs clarity. It needs structure. It needs a question with boundaries.

   But authentic leadership lives in the gray zone, the *both/and,* the tension between what's smart and what's right. And that's where generalists shine—sitting in uncertainty long enough to see what others miss.

   It can't make moral calls.

   AI can tell you what people usually do. It can't tell you what they ought to do.

   There's no algorithm for integrity.

   Ethical decisions require judgment, especially when the stakes are high and the rules don't fit. That's not a software problem—it's a human one.

2. **It can't see the long view.**

   AI is trained on the past. Even its predictions are built on yesterday's data. It doesn't have vision, memory, or understanding of how change unfolds across time, systems, and generations.

3. **It can't lead with lived experience.**

   AI doesn't know what it feels like to fire someone.

To build trust.

To walk into a broken team and try to rebuild something real.

Leadership is embodied. Emotional. It lives in the space between people. You can't outsource that.

The Human System Around the Machine

So here's the fundamental shift: The machine is no longer just a tool—it's part of the system we lead.

That means we need leaders who don't just use AI but who know how to wrap it in wisdom. Leaders who can:

- Ask better questions.
- Spot what's missing.
- Interpret results with discernment.

Sense when to hit send—and when to hit pause.
That's what generalists do.
We don't just look at the output. We look at the impact.
We don't just chase efficiency. We protect meaning.
We don't just plug in the machine. We design the system around it.

Because without human judgment, the system will default to speed. To short-term logic. To whatever is cheapest, fastest, and most obvious.

And let me tell you—that's how innovative companies make dumb decisions.

So no, I'm not anti-AI. But I am very pro-human.

And if you're reading this, it's because you're the kind of leader who doesn't just want to stay relevant—you want to remain responsible. You want to lead well, not just fast. And you want to keep your hands on the wheel in a world that's accelerating whether we're ready or not.

The machine has a role.

But we still need a human at the wheel.

Leadership Cue:

Where might the machine's limits require a sharper human lens in your next big call?

Chapter 2

The Rise of the System Thinker

UNDERSTANDING THE LIMITATIONS of AI naturally leads us to a critical insight: AI isn't just a tool; it's reshaping our organizational systems. **To lead effectively, we need a new way of seeing—enter the rise of the system thinker.**

There's a mistake I see over and over again in leadership conversations about AI.

People keep talking about what the machine can do.

They should be talking about how it fits into the system.

Because AI isn't just another tool. It's a force multiplier. It doesn't just change workflows. It changes the conditions. It shifts power. It rewrites incentives. And if you're not paying attention to the system around it, you'll solve the wrong problems faster.

That's where generalists come in.

We don't just look at the task. We look at the context.

We don't just see the input and output. We see the ripple.

We're not trying to predict everything—we're trying to read the whole damn map.

---

*The future belongs to the system thinker
who knows what the model means.*

Specialists Optimize. Generalists Orchestrate.

In a world of increasingly powerful tools, the job of the generalist leader isn't to master every input. It's to see the relationships between them. To understand where feedback loops live. Where failure points hide. Where an innovative solution in one silo creates a mess somewhere else.

You've seen it—a brilliant AI model for hiring decisions built without a single voice from HR, DEI, or legal. It looks great until it starts amplifying bias and exposing the company to lawsuits. Why? Because nobody was watching the system— they were watching the model.

This is the cost of tunnel vision in a systems world.

And this is where generalist leadership starts to shine.

The Machine Lives in the Middle. You Have to See the Whole.

AI is excellent at helping you with a slice of the problem. A single process. A narrow set of variables. But most real-world challenges don't live in a clean slice.

They live in the intersections:
Between technology and culture.
Between operations and ethics.
Between scale and story.

If you're not looking across those boundaries, you're not leading—you're reacting.

Generalists are built to do more than react. We're built to integrate. To interpret. To see one decision not as a single act but as part of a larger choreography. That's why I call it symphonic leadership. You don't just play louder—you conduct across disciplines. You shape how the whole thing moves.

Complexity Isn't the Enemy. Disconnection Is.

Look, complexity isn't what sinks organizations. What sinks them is siloed thinking inside a complex system. When marketing does one thing, ops does another, and tech does a third, no one sees how everything collides downstream.

AI won't fix that. On the contrary, it can make it worse by giving every function more power to move fast without coordinating with anyone else.

That's the trap.

The generalist leader sees it coming.

We slow the knee-jerk response. We ask:

"Where does this decision land three steps from now?"

"What does this change mean to the people it wasn't built for?"

"What happens when the data's clean but the story is off?"

That's not soft leadership. That's *systems* leadership. And it's what keeps the machine from running off a cliff.

How System Thinkers Lead Differently

Here's how generalist leaders stand apart in AI-heavy environments:

1. They zoom out first.

   While others jump to fix, they ask, "What's really going on here?"

2. They listen wide.

   They don't just pull the technical team, they bring in voices from the edge—people who see the impact before the dashboard ever will.

3. They name the tension.

   System thinkers aren't afraid to say, "This works for one team and screws another." They surface trade-offs early before they become lawsuits, burnout, or broken trust.

4. They lead across disciplines.

   Not by pretending to be an expert in everything but by building bridges, asking sharp questions, and making sure no lane drives blind.

The Future Belongs to the Integrators

We're heading into a future where every decision touches tech, culture, ethics, economics, and emotion—all at once.

If you're only fluent in one of those lanes, you'll miss what's coming.

But if you can connect them? Then you can think in layers, hold tension, and see patterns across the mess.

Then you're not just ready for the future, you're prepared to lead it.

The machine will keep getting faster.

Your job isn't to outrun it.

Your job is to ensure it's moving in the right direction, at the right cost, with the right consequences, inside the right system.

That's what a generalist leader does.

And that's why the future of leadership doesn't belong to the specialist who can code the model.

It belongs to the system thinker who knows what the model means.

Leadership Cue:

What system dynamic are you overlooking that could change your leadership strategy?

Chapter 3

The End of the Single-Lane Career

THINKING IN SYSTEMS changes more than our decisions—it changes what leadership looks like entirely. The era where careers neatly fit into single lanes is ending, demanding leaders who can integrate and navigate across multiple disciplines.

There Was a Time When Picking a Lane Made Sense

You went deep, stayed loyal to a discipline, and climbed the ranks. Your title said everything anyone needed to know. That model worked—when the world moved slowly, the problems were mostly predictable, and the rules didn't change mid-game.

But let's be honest: That world's gone.

AI didn't kill the single-lane career, it just exposed how fragile it already was.

Now we're working on live systems. Jobs evolve overnight, and skills expire faster than degrees. Leaders aren't rewarded for sticking to their lane—they're expected to navigate across it.

Welcome to the era of the multidisciplinary career.

And whether you chose it or stumbled into it, this shift is permanent.

The Specialist Identity Is Under Pressure

Let's not confuse this: we still need specialists. Deep knowledge still matters. You still want the heart surgeon who's done the same procedure a thousand times. You want engineers who know exactly how and why something works.

However, the value of a specialist increasingly depends on how well they integrate with the system around them.

And here's the truth no one wants to say: AI encroaches on the specialist's comfort zone.

AI is already performing those tasks faster than most human experts in writing, coding, drafting, and diagnosing—not better in all cases, but fast enough to upend the value ladder. Specialists who once owned a domain now share it with machines that don't sleep and don't hesitate.

So where's the advantage now?

It's not in being the person who knows.

It's in being the person who can navigate, integrate, and adapt.

Generalists Aren't Wandering, They're Patterning

If you've ever been told you were "scattered," "unfocused," or "trying to do too much," I want you to hear this clearly:

Those were never the problem. You were just ahead of schedule.

The world wasn't ready for multidisciplinarians.

Now it doesn't work without them.

The generalists I know—real generalists, not dabblers—don't drift aimlessly. They cross-pollinate. They build internal maps. They don't just switch lanes. They see how lanes connect.

That's what this chapter is about: reframing the idea that having multiple lanes is a liability.

In an AI-powered workplace, the ability to draw from multiple disciplines, read across perspectives, and apply lived experience separates the conductor from the technician.

The age of the single-lane career is over, but that doesn't mean people need to become something they're not.

The Myth of Mastery, Revisited

In *The Generalist's Advantage,* I wrote:

Being a generalist does not require a deep dive into any one field. What you sacrifice in depth you make up for in breadth—and that's where great things happen.

That still holds. But now, there's more urgency to it.

Because in the AI world, deep isn't enough.

What matters is whether you can move laterally or connect your depth to something bigger.

The person who only knows how to do one thing? They're at the mercy of disruption.

The person who knows how their lane affects five others? They're leading the redesign.

How the Career Model is Breaking— and Rebuilding

Let's look at how careers are shifting in real time:

- Modular portfolios are replacing linear career paths. People aren't staying in one role for 20 years—they're building bodies of work across contexts.

- Credentials are losing their weight. Lived experience, pattern fluency, and adaptability are what teams rely on.

- Expertise is no longer enough to lead. What matters now is the ability to interpret, align, and guide across disciplines, tools, and timelines.

If you're a generalist, this is your moment—not because the system now rewards your resume, but because it requires your thinking.

The AI Era Needs a Different Kind of Credibility

Here's the new leadership math:

The more AI can do, the more humans need to know how to connect, contextualize, and create meaning.

You don't have to be the fastest. You have to be the most aware.

- Can you see how a tool will land inside the culture?
- Can you spot when a data-driven insight is morally off?
- Can you read between the disciplines and ask the question no one else thought to ask?

That's credibility now.

That's what the new career path demands.

From Career Path to Career Mosaic

Let's pull a thread from *Hold the Horizon:* the idea that a generalist career isn't a ladder—it's a mosaic.

Each lane you've walked, each field you've explored, and each chapter you thought was a detour is part of a larger pattern.

What AI can't replicate is that interwoven depth.

You're not less valuable because your path wasn't traditional. You're more valuable because your map is richer than a resume. You bring context, intuition, and perspective. You see what others miss.

This Isn't Reinvention, It's Reclamation.

The age of the single-lane career is over, but that doesn't mean people need to become something they're not. For generalists, this isn't about changing. It's about owning what we've already been doing—and doing it out loud.

That mix of disciplines you've carried?

That strange career arc that never made sense on paper?

That ability to walk into chaos and start making sense?

That's the value. That's the edge. That's the leadership we need now.

It's not a glitch.

It's your design.

Leadership Cue:

How might your diverse experience help connect the dots others miss?

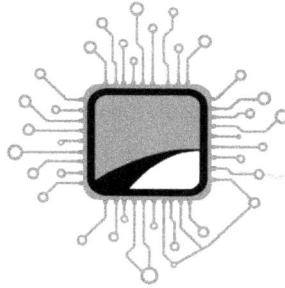

PART II
THE GENERALIST EDGE
IN THE AGE OF AI

The machine has changed the conditions,
but leadership does not depend on the speed
of the tools. It belongs to those who can
hold ambiguity, lead with judgment,
and see the whole system.

In Part I, we've clarified the changing landscape leaders face in the age of AI. We've distinguished precisely at what AI excels—speed, scale, and data-driven tasks—and identified the critical leadership functions it cannot fulfill, such as moral judgment, ambiguity management, and contextual understanding. We've also recognized the rising necessity of system thinkers and generalist leaders who integrate multiple perspectives.

Finally, we've declared the end of single-lane careers, emphasizing that future-ready leadership requires navigating complexity by connecting disciplines, experiences, and insights. Now, in Part II, we move forward into practical strategies and clear frameworks to leverage the unique advantages of generalist leadership in this new terrain.

Chapter 4

Synthesis Over Search

WE'VE LAID OUT the new terrain. Now it's time to explore exactly how generalist leaders thrive in this complex landscape. The chapters ahead offer tactical insights to strengthen your leadership advantage in an AI-driven world.

Generalists Don't Just Collect Information— We Connect It

In a world where anyone can find the answer, the value lies in knowing what to do with it. That's what it means to lead beyond the prompt.

In AI, the people who can find answers aren't rare. Everyone can find answers now.

You don't need a researcher. You need a reframer. You need someone who knows what the answer means in context.

That's what synthesis is: seeing the whole pattern—not just the data points.

Search is passive. It asks, "What's already out there?"

Synthesis is active. It asks, "What does this connect to, and what should we do with it?"

The Machine Retrieves; We Interpret

Ask AI a question, and you'll get a response. Sometimes it's even useful. But here's what it can't do:

It doesn't know which data points matter.

It doesn't know what's noise and what's a signal.

It doesn't know when the correct answer is the wrong move.

That's *our* job.

This is where generalist leadership becomes more important, not less. In an age where everyone has access to the same information, what separates leaders isn't knowledge—it's judgment.

Let the machine run the search.
You handle the synthesis.

You're Not Just Prompting a Machine, You're Framing a Problem

AI doesn't generate ideas from anywhere. It responds to the question you ask. So if your question is too narrow, shallow, or disconnected, the output will reflect it.

That's why generalists are often the most valuable people in the room. We ask the questions others don't. We see across lanes. We hold context. We know when a sharp answer doesn't fit a messy problem. Our ability to ask the right questions, to see connections where others see only data, is what sets us apart in the age of AI.

Let the machine run the search.
You handle the synthesis.

Don't Confuse Speed with Clarity

AI is fast. That's not in question. But what shows up fast isn't always what moves the needle.

You can generate twenty options in seconds. That doesn't mean any of them are helpful. You still need someone who can read the situation, spot the implications, and decide what matters.

And let's be honest—how many meetings have you attended where more information wasn't the problem?

We don't need more input amidst the flood of information. We need people who can filter, connect, and decide. It's not the quantity of information we have, but the quality of our interpretation and decision-making that matters most.

We need people who can filter, connect, and decide.

How Generalists Practice Synthesis

Let's call it what it is: pattern work.

It's how we link a phrase from a finance report to a morale issue we noticed last week. It's when we ask a question no one else does—not because it's brilliant, but because we're tracking the system, not the silo.

Here's how synthesis tends to show up in real time:

You hear what's being said—and what isn't.
You name the second-order impact before it hits.
You translate insights across teams that don't talk
to each other.

You spot when something feels "off" before data proves it.

That's not magic. That's synthesis.

That's generalist muscle memory in action.

The GENERALIST Leadership Model

As we explore how generalists lead through synthesis, it's helpful to name the leadership traits that define this approach. The GENERALIST Model captures the essential mindsets needed to lead in the AI era:

G: Grounded in vision

E: Ethical by design

N: Navigates ambiguity

E: Empathizes across systems

R: Reflects before acting

A: Aligns technology with purpose

L: Listens beyond the surface

I: Integrates across silos

S: Synthesizes complexity

T: Trusts the long view

This model is more than an acronym—it's a practical anchor for navigating AI with clarity and conscience. Refer to it when you're evaluating tools, framing questions, or conducting the human system around the machine.

The Best Ideas Don't Come from Search Bars

They come from unexpected intersections. From when something you learned when you worked in logistics applies to your current leadership of the HR department, or when you recall something from a half-remembered psychology concept and connect it to a policy problem. It's combining lived experience with just enough outside insight to see something afresh.

You won't get that from ChatGPT.

You get that from you.

Because you've lived in enough lanes to see how they fit together.

What This Means for Your Teams

You're not the only one feeling the pressure. Your people are watching the tools evolve and wondering where they fit. Some are terrified, some are in denial, and most just don't know what to do with the noise.

Your job isn't to know everything the machine can do.

Your job is to create space for human thinking—real, integrative, collaborative sense-making.

Synthesis isn't a solo act. It's cultural.

Build teams that don't just divide up tasks. Build reams that connect the dots.

Hold the Pattern, Not Just the Answer

Let AI search the web.

Let generalists search for meaning.

That's how you lead in this new terrain.

When things speed up, we don't default to faster. We default to clearer.

When the system gets smarter, we don't check out. We zoom out.

We lead the integration.

That's the real job now. And it's not going anywhere.

Leadership Cue:

What's one situation today that needs synthesis, not just search?

Chapter 5

Leading the Human–Machine Collaboration

We've seen why synthesis outperforms search when complexity is high. But what does it mean practically? How do you lead effectively when humans and machines must collaborate closely?

The Machine Isn't Your Rival

It's your amplifier.

You'll lose if you try to compete with it on speed, scale, or recall. That's not a knock on you—it's just not where humans win.

Where you win is in how you lead the whole system.

That includes the tools. The people. The consequences. The timing. The context.

That's the leadership AI doesn't—and can't—do.

Because while the machine executes, you still direct.

And if you're a generalist leader, this is your moment. You don't need to be an engineer or a data scientist. You need to know how to keep the system aligned when the tools move faster than the people.

You're conducting a system, not pressing a button.

You Don't Need to Know How AI Works, You Just Need to Know What It's For

Some leaders feel stuck because they think they're not relevant if they're not fluent in machine learning.

Your job isn't to build the model.

Your job is to understand the implications of using it.

Where will this tool fit?

What does it change?

Who's included in the decision and who's affected by it?

What does it free up—and what does it quietly erode?

This isn't about catching up to the machine. It's about keeping humans in the loop, not in the dark.

Leading People Through Tools They Don't Yet Trust

Half your team doesn't understand AI, and the other half doesn't trust it.

Some are excited, some are scared, and some are burned out from another wave of tech they didn't ask for. If you try to force this through like a software upgrade, you'll get quiet, real, and disruptive resistance.

So don't lead with the tool. Lead with the why.

Why this tool?

Why now?

Why does it matter in the ways we work, serve, or decide?

Build trust in the process. Share what it's for and what it's not. Be transparent about the risks. Acknowledge what you don't know. Let people pressure-test the plan.

People don't need a flawless rollout. They need to feel seen.

What Generalist Leaders Do Differently in AI-Heavy Environments

The specialists build it. The generalists keep it in orbit.

Here's how you lead the collaboration, not just the adoption:

You link disciplines.

You ensure tech, ops, legal, and people are all in the same conversation. Because AI won't just affect one of them—it will change the balance across all of them.

You lead with judgment.

Just because something can be automated doesn't mean it should be. You make the call when human discernment matters more than machine efficiency.

You monitor the ripple.

You ask, "What makes this shift easier? What does it make harder? What do we lose in the handoff?" Most people miss those second-order effects. You don't.

You create space for questions.

Not everyone will feel confident right away. Let them

be uncertain. Let them push back. That's how absolute alignment happens.

You integrate, not just implement.

You don't just drop the tool in. You help your team figure out where it fits, how it shifts the workflow, and what it frees them up to focus on instead.

You're Conducting a System, Not Pressing a Button

Too many leaders think of AI as a one-time decision—choose the tool, turn it on, and move on.

That's not how this works.

You're not leading a tool. You're leading a living system that now includes AI. It's not static. It responds. It evolves. And the leadership model must evolve with it.

Think like a conductor, not a technician.

The system only works when the timing, context, and people sync. That's not something you can outsource to an algorithm. That's your role—and it's more important now than ever.

Use the Machine, Keep the Mind

Let AI handle what it's good at.

- The repetition
- The math
- The surface-level draft
- The crunching, sorting, recommending

But you? You hold the decisions. You hold the tone. You hold the long view.

AI won't forget anything. But it also won't remember what matters.

Leadership Cue:

How can you guide collaboration without getting lost in tools?

Chapter 6

Context is King

SUCCESSFULLY MANAGING HUMAN–machine collaboration requires more than strategy—it demands context. **Context shapes every decision, reminding us that leadership is fundamentally about understanding people and their environments.**

AI processes data at lightning speed, identifies patterns, and offers solutions that would take humans much longer to compute. But here's the catch: AI doesn't understand context.

It doesn't grasp the nuances of a team's dynamics, the history behind a company's culture, or the subtle cues in a client's hesitation. AI does not have emotional intelligence. After all, it's still just a machine.

When teams are under stress, it's often the smallest cues—a glance, a hesitation—that guide how leaders respond. AI misses these. That's why human leadership is essential where emotion, trust, and team cohesion live. We, as human-centric leaders—with our knack for feeling the undercurrents and reading between the lines—can really guide things when subtlety matters. That's where human leadership becomes irreplaceable.

Understanding the Bigger Picture

As a generalist leader, your strength lies in seeing the whole picture. You connect dots across disciplines, understand the interplay between departments, and anticipate the ripple effects of decisions.

AI will map your fastest route. Just like when you get in your car and tell Waze where you want to go, its focus is always on getting you where you're going.

It does not stop to smell the roses or consider the excitement of the journey itself.

The Human Element

Consider a scenario where AI recommends downsizing a department based on performance metrics. On paper, it makes sense. But you know that department is the heart of company culture, fostering innovation and morale. AI does not understand that the people in that department may be the heart and soul of your operation. You can instruct AI with that information—but it won't understand it. It will process it as data. Eliminating that department could have long-term detrimental effects that AI can't predict.

It is the job of the human to look at everything through a human lens. AI cannot do that.

AI can offer information, but it can't provide wisdom.

Real-World Thoughts:

In Southeast Asia, organizations that invest in strong AI governance frameworks are seeing clear benefits. A 2024 Deloitte report highlighted that companies with mature AI oversight experience higher staff engagement with AI solutions, while organizations lacking robust governance face growing employee concerns about security vulnerabilities and privacy breaches, contributing to a significant trust gap.[2]

Complementing this, research from Great Place To Work found that when employees are actively involved in AI implementation decisions and receive targeted training, they are significantly more likely to embrace AI initiatives. This approach not only improves operational efficiency but also preserves cultural cohesion and trust within organizations.[3]

Together, these findings underscore the critical importance of balancing technical advancement with human-centered leadership—ensuring that AI-driven efficiencies do not come at the expense of organizational trust and alignment.

Incorporate AI into your decision-making process, but don't let it dictate your choices. Use it as a tool, not a crutch—balance data-driven insights with your intuition and understanding, taking responsibility for the final decision.

---

[2] AI at a Crossroads | Deloitte Asia Pacific, https://www.deloitte.com/global/en/offices/apac/perspectives/apac-trustworthy-ai-report.html, 'Fewer than two-thirds of organizations in SEA believe their employees have the capabilities to use AI responsibly,' 2024.

[3] Great Place To Work, 'How to Boost Employee Trust in AI,' 2024. Leading with Context, Kitterman, Ted. https://www.greatplacetowork.com/resources/blog/report-how-to-boost-employee-trust-in-ai?utm_source=chatgpt.com

Remember that context is about everything that has happened in the past, the present, and what we foresee for the future. That is the human element.

AI can offer information, but it can't provide wisdom.

AI does not possess the understanding and emotional intelligence from the human experience. As a generalist leader, your ability to contextualize, empathize, and force consequences from a human standpoint is invaluable.

Human insight, with its ability to understand context and empathize, trumps logarithms every time. It is that insight that will guide you through complexity and change, validating the role of human decision-making in the age of AI.

Leadership Cue:

**What context matters most in your current
toughest decision?**

Chapter7

You Can't Google Your Way to Wisdom

WHILE CONTEXT IS crucial, it's also linked to something deeper: wisdom. Let's clarify the vital distinction between finding information and making wise decisions—because true wisdom can't simply be Googled or prompted.

You Can Find Facts in Seconds

You can find trends, patterns, and case studies.

But you can't Google—or prompt—your way to leadership judgment.

Here's what I mean.

Suppose you asked an AI:

Prompt:

```
"Should my company lay off 10% of
employees if financial models predict
a 15% cost savings next quarter?"
```

You'll get an answer that sounds like this:

AI Response:

> "If laying off 10% of employees will result in a 15% cost savings, and no significant operational risks are identified, it may be a sound financial decision. It is recommended to evaluate the impact on morale, brand reputation, and future hiring needs. Clear communication strategies are critical to minimize disruption."

Sounds reasonable, right?

Efficient. Logical. Covered the basics.

But here's what it didn't say:

- Which employees are you losing?
- What critical knowledge walks out the door with them?
- What long-term trust are you sacrificing inside your culture?
- How will this decision affect your ability to hire the next time?

Is the short-term gain worth the long-term erosion of your organization's soul?

No model can hold all that.

Because it's not a math problem. It's a leadership call.

It's a choice about who you are, not just what you save.

***You can't Google—or prompt—your way
to leadership judgment.***

This Is Where Generalists Step In

You don't just look at cost savings.

You hold the weight of reputation, trust, resilience.

You don't just check operational risks—you think about the second, third, and fourth ripple effects across the entire system.

AI will give you an answer.

You still have to decide what matters.

That's why in a world of faster tools, generalists aren't getting squeezed out.

They're getting called up.

Generalists Don't Just Solve, They Frame

If you walk away from this chapter remembering one thing, let it be this:

The leaders who frame the right questions—and interpret the answers—will shape the future.

That's the edge you already have.

And the future's going to need a lot more of it.

When the Machine Gives You an Answer, Ask These Five Follow-Ups Before You Act

1. Who is impacted beyond what the numbers show?

2. What second- and third-order consequences could unfold from this decision?

3. Are we solving the root problem—or just treating a symptom?

4. How does this decision align (or clash) with our values, culture, or mission?

5. What critical information might be missing from the model's assumptions?

Before you act on an AI-generated recommendation, slow down and walk through these questions. The machine can calculate, but it can't see the full system. That's your job.

Leadership Cue:

**What question do you need to reframe
before you act?**

Chapter 8

The Ethical Compass

WISDOM NATURALLY CONNECTS to ethics. Knowing the right thing to do isn't just a data-driven task—it's a moral one. Leaders must hold tightly to an ethical compass, especially when the system pushes speed and efficiency above all else.

AI Will Tell You What You Can Do; It Won't Tell You What You Should Do

Leadership isn't just about finding the efficient path. It's about choosing the right one.

And in a world where machines are making faster, cleaner, smarter-looking recommendations, the temptation to disconnect from that responsibility will only grow. After all, if the system suggested it—how bad could it be?

Pretty bad if nobody's thinking past the numbers.

That's why generalist leaders are essential right now:

We don't just execute decisions.

We carry the consequences.

AI will tell you what you can do. It won't tell you what you should do.

When the System Says Yes and Leadership Says No

AI is optimizing for whatever you point it at—efficiency, engagement, profitability, speed. It doesn't know when to pump the brakes.

It doesn't know:

- When a smart move erodes trust.
- When a fast rollout damages your culture.
- When squeezing a little more profit guts the loyalty you've spent a decade earning.

The system can clear the path, but it can't see the cliff at the end of it.

You can.

Or at least—you're supposed to.

What Happens Without a Human Ethical Check?

We're already seeing the consequences.

- Companies implementing AI hiring models that quietly reinforce biases they didn't catch.
- Algorithms recommending cuts or restructures that look great on paper but destroy the underlying culture.

- Layoffs, product shifts, or marketing campaigns that miss the human impact entirely.

Not because people were malicious, but because they trusted the optimization more than their own ethical compass.

No machine will ever stop you and say, "This might be wrong for reasons you can't quantify."

That's the leadership that endures.

That's human work.

The Role of the Generalist Leader: Ethical Framing at Speed

When things are moving fast, it's tempting to think you don't have time to slow down for critical questions.

But those are the questions that will keep your team—your reputation—your integrity—intact.

That's why generalists, who are trained to see across lanes, across systems, and across timeframes, are so critical in this moment.

You see the side effects most people miss. You see the trade-offs they haven't yet thought through.

You're not slowing things down to be cautious. You're protecting something bigger than quarterly results.

AI Doesn't Carry Blame; *You* Do

At the end of the day, the machine doesn't attend the all-hands meeting and explain why trust is broken.

The machine doesn't deal with the town halls, the resignations, the lawsuits, the "I thought we were better than this" conversations.

You do.

Leadership isn't about executing faster. It's about absorbing the weight of decisions that affect real lives.

You can use every tool in the world, but you can't offload your ethical judgment—not to the machine, not to anyone.

Steering the System Still Requires a Human Hand

You don't have to be perfect. You don't have to predict every ripple.

But you do have to care.

You have to slow down just long enough to ask:

- Does this decision align with who we say we are?

- If I had to explain this to the people it affects, would I stand behind it?

AI will give you options. You decide what's acceptable.

That's human leadership. And that's why, no matter how fast the system gets, we still need a human to make the right call.

The Generalist's Quick Ethics Check Before Acting on AI Recommendations

1. Who is impacted beyond the immediate numbers?

2. What long-term trust or reputation could be affected?

3. What critical risks might the system not account for?

4. Does this decision align with our values—or just our metrics?

5. Would I be willing to explain this decision directly to those it affects?

Before you accept a machine's suggestion, slow down and walk through these five questions. Ethical leadership isn't just knowing what's possible. It's choosing what's right.

Leadership Cue:

What principle are you protecting before speed takes over?

(See Appendix A for a full ethics checklist to guide decision-making.)

Chapter 9

Conducting the Symphony

ETHICS ANCHOR THE system, but someone still needs to manage its rhythm and flow. True leadership is orchestration: coordinating diverse elements, including people and AI, into a coherent whole—much like conducting a symphony.

Leadership in an AI-Driven World Isn't About Controlling Every Detail; It's About Conducting the Whole System

There's a rhythm to organizations now—one that's faster, more layered, less predictable.

You've got AI tools moving at speed.

You've got specialists operating deep in their own lanes.

You've got teams adjusting to new expectations on the fly.

And it's easy for it all to splinter if someone isn't holding the broader shape.

That's your job.

You're not there to micromanage every piece.

You're there to make sure everything still plays in time, still builds toward something that sounds like music—not noise.

Why Orchestration, Not Control

The old model of leadership said: Set the plan. Enforce the process. Push it through.

That's dead.

The new model demands something different:

Adaptability.
Connection.
Timing.
Trust.

You have to actively conduct, adjusting to the dynamics in real time.

Conducting isn't about knowing every note. It's about holding the integrity of the whole piece.

The Elements You're Conducting Now

Leading across human-machine systems means you're no longer just managing people.

You're managing:

- Human capability (experience, intuition, judgment).

- Machine capacity (speed, data, automation).

- Organizational rhythm (culture, urgency, pressure).

- External forces (market shifts, public expectations, societal impact).

Each one moves at a different tempo. Each one hears the beat differently.

You conduct the whole thing—not perfectly, but intentionally.

Leadership in an AI-driven world isn't about controlling every detail. It's about conducting the whole system.

How Generalists Lead the Symphony

Generalists are built for this moment. You're wired to:

- Hear when something's off before it shows up in the numbers.

- Notice when two groups are talking past each other.

- Sense when the team is moving fast but losing the thread.

- Hold competing goals in tension without forcing false choices.

When you lead that way—when you conduct the moving parts instead of forcing them—you create something AI can't replicate:

Coherence. Meaning. Trust.

You make sure the system doesn't just move. It moves with purpose.

You Don't Have to Be the Loudest Voice; You Have to Set the Tone

Real conductors don't scream directions. They shape the flow with subtle signals, small corrections, well-timed cues.

You don't have to dominate every meeting. You don't have to out-expert the experts or out-speed the machines.

You have to know:

- When to slow the tempo.
- When to push the volume.
- When to let the system breathe.

You don't control the players. You create the conditions for them to play their best work together.

Symphonies Don't Conduct Themselves

Without leadership, even talented systems fall apart.

- Teams drift into silos.
- Tools get misused or abandoned.
- Strategy gets replaced by speed.
- Cultures decay quietly under the surface.

The machine can automate a lot. But it can't hold a vision across difference. It can't listen for coherence. It can't balance urgency with care.

You can.

And that's why, in a world full of faster tools, the leaders who know how to conduct the symphony will be the ones who hold the future together.

The Generalist Leader's Conductor Cues: Five Moments to Watch For in AI-Human Systems

1. When the technology outpaces the team's understanding—pause and realign.

2. When specialists retreat into silos—bridge the spaces between them.

3. When data looks clean but tension rises in the room—listen to the human signals.

4. When speed starts replacing sense—slow the tempo before you lose coherence.

5. When wins feel hollow—re-anchor everyone to the real purpose behind the work.

The conductor's job isn't to force uniformity. It's to keep different parts moving toward a common sound, a common story. That's leadership now.

Leadership Cue:

What part of your system needs conducting— not control?

Chapter 10

Speaking Beyond the Prompt

ARE YOU SPEAKING to Lead or Speaking for Content?

Orchestrating systems effectively requires precise, intentional communication. But not all speech moves systems forward—leaders must distinguish clearly between speaking to lead and merely speaking for content.

In an AI-accelerated world where communication floods every channel, it's easy to mistake "more words" for real leadership.

But leaders must hold firm on one crucial distinction:

Speaking to lead is different from speaking for content.

And in a world flooded with content, it's the leaders who learn to speak with true intention that will shape what matters next.

AI can flood the room with knowledge, but only a leader can move the room with meaning.

AI Has Given Everyone a Microphone

AI has democratized access to knowledge, content, and "smart" talking points. In meetings, in memos, and in strategy sessions, it's easier than ever to sound informed.

But there's a hidden trap: When everyone can generate content, speaking itself can become confused with leading.

Specialists thrive on content—on delivering depth, data, and details.

But generalists? Generalists are responsible for something bigger.

Generalists must integrate, orchestrate, and keep the entire system moving forward with clarity, humanity, and vision.

That means knowing why you speak—and what you are anchoring—matters more than ever.

Speaking for Content

Content speaks to fill a feed.

Content speaks to showcase expertise.

Content speaks to show up in the room.

But without awareness and integration, content becomes noise—even if it's factually correct.

AI can give anyone enough knowledge to "sound smart."

But knowledge alone doesn't move systems. It doesn't build trust. It doesn't connect.

It informs.

It updates.

It fills space.

And if we're not careful, it dilutes leadership.

Speaking to Lead

Leadership communication isn't about proving you know something.

It's about moving the system with what you say.

Speaking to lead asks:

- What needs integration?
- What tension needs naming?

How do I keep this conversation anchored to what matters? When you speak to lead, you're not just contributing.

You're conducting.

You're connecting.

You're carrying forward.

Speaking to lead requires sensing the room, reading the signals beneath the surface, and choosing words that guide, not just fill.

Why This Matters More in the Age of AI

In a world where AI can generate information faster than thought, leadership isn't about who knows the most.

It's about who can:

- Sense when information is enough.
- See when knowledge needs to be connected, not just presented.
- Move a team, not just fill a file.

Someone with AI-generated knowledge but no ability to read a room, connect dots, or sense timing is ineffective.

Leadership requires something deeper:

- Awareness of system needs.

- Alignment to purpose.

- Judgment about when to speak, when to listen, and when to steer.

AI can give you content, but it can't give you connection.

AI can give you answers, but it can't tell you which answers the room is ready to hear—or which ones they most need.

That's human work.

That's leadership work.

Leadership Reminder

Before you speak, ask yourself:

- Am I speaking to add content—or to move the system?

- Am I helping to integrate, or just adding to the noise?

- Am I leading—or just contributing?

In a world where everyone can speak, the leaders who know why they speak—and speak with system-level intention—will shape the future.

Because the future doesn't just need more content.

It needs humans to guide us with purpose.

Leadership Cue:

What conversation this week needs leadership, not just information?

Chapter 11

Holding the Horizon

UNDERSTANDING PURPOSEFUL SPEECH leads us to the heart of generalist leadership: holding the horizon. Amid noise, speed, and distractions, leaders must maintain a steady, clear vision of the long-term path ahead.

In a World Obsessed with Speed, There's Real Power in the Ability to Hold Steady

It's easy to chase what's urgent. It's easy to chase the next tool, the next trend, the next demand that screams the loudest.

But leadership isn't about chasing.

It's about holding the horizon.

It's about seeing beyond the next quarter, the next rollout, the next wave of noise. It's about keeping your eyes locked on where you're actually trying to go—even when the system keeps throwing new distractions in your path.

And that's something no machine will ever be built to do.

Holding the horizon means keeping your leadership tied to something bigger than the latest push.

Speed Isn't Strategy I: Navigating Economic Pressures

Leaders face mounting pressure to automate faster, optimize aggressively, and prioritize efficiency at the expense of human values. Budgets will tighten. Expectations will rise.

Holding the horizon doesn't mean ignoring these realities. It means making human-centered decisions even when speed looks easier and cost-cutting looks smarter.

Leadership in the age of AI will mean advocating for what lasts—not just what costs less in the next quarter.

Speed Isn't Strategy II: Navigating Boardroom Pressures

Boards and investors often prioritize ROI, efficiency, and rapid gains, pushing for aggressive AI adoption. Yet as a CEO, you understand that speed without trust, or efficiency without alignment, erodes strategic value. In advocating for human-centered leadership, emphasize long-term resilience and stakeholder trust. Frame your leadership not as resisting innovation, but as ensuring innovation strengthens your organization's future story.

In boardrooms, the conversation won't just be about ethics. It will be about costs, returns, and competition. Real leadership will mean holding the human center steady even when external pressures push for faster, cheaper, easier.

AI Moves Faster Than We Do

It can optimize for the shortest path, the biggest gain, the most efficient answer. But it can't ask:

- What happens five moves from now?
- What's the story we're building—not just the product we're launching?
- Are we reinforcing what matters or just reacting to what's loud?

Because when the race is constant, it's not the fastest who win. It's the ones who remember what they're racing toward.

Seeing the Second and Third Horizons

Good leadership doesn't just solve for what's directly ahead. It looks for what's coming next—and what might come after that.

Holding the horizon means asking:

- If we win this quarter, what might we lose long-term?
- If we roll out this change, what expectations do we set for the future?
- If we train the system to prioritize this, what habits do we reinforce down the line?

Most people are heads down. Generalists are built to keep scanning.

You're not just solving today's problem. You're shaping tomorrow's reality.

The Machine Can't Tell You What's Worth Building

AI can predict a trend line. It can automate a response. It can optimize a process.

But it can't tell you:

- What kind of organization you want to build.
- What kind of trust you want to earn.
- What kind of future you want to live in.

Those decisions don't come from data.

They come from vision.

They come from people willing to slow down, step back, and ask bigger questions—even when it's easier to just speed up and check another box.

The Weight—and the Gift—of the Horizon

Holding the horizon isn't easy.

It means sometimes being the one saying:

- Wait. Let's think this through.
- This solves the short-term, but creates a bigger long-term mess.
- Is this who we want to be, or just what's easiest right now?

It means carrying weight when others want to travel light.
It means carrying vision when others want to move faster.
But it's also a gift.

Because the leaders who hold the horizon shape more than outcomes.

They shape trust.

They shape culture.

They shape meaning.

They leave places better than they found them.

You're Not Just Steering the System, You're Holding Its Future

The machine will get faster. The tools will keep evolving.

But the need for human leadership—the kind that sees past the immediate, holds complexity, and chooses with conscience—that's only going to grow.

Generalists aren't just ready for this future. We're built for it.

Because in a world of instant answers, the ones who can still see, still sense, and still steer toward something bigger?

They're not just leading teams.

They're holding the horizon for all of us.

Five Questions for Generalists Who Hold the Horizon in the AI Era

- What future impact am I responsible for beyond this immediate decision?

- Are we reinforcing the right habits—or just reacting to short-term wins?

- Who will inherit the culture we are shaping right now?

- What unintended consequences could ripple from this choice five years from now?
- Does this move align with the future story we want to tell?

Holding the horizon isn't about predicting everything correctly. It's about keeping your leadership tied to something bigger than the latest push. That's how generalists lead systems—and shape futures worth living in.

Leadership Cue:

What vision do you hold steady when others rush?

Keep the Horizon Human

The World Isn't Slowing Down.

And not every system built in haste will be kind, wise, or just. Leaders will need more than vision. They'll need resilience.

The systems are getting smarter. The noise is getting louder.

And the pressure to move faster, to automate more, to trust the machine just a little bit further—that's not going away.

But here's the part we can't afford to forget:

- Speed doesn't replace judgment.

- Automation doesn't replace leadership.

- And optimization doesn't replace meaning.

It's easy to get caught chasing the next tool, the next metric, the next shortcut.

It's harder—and more important—to stay human. To keep leading like it still matters.

Because it does.

Speed doesn't replace judgment. Automation doesn't replace leadership. Optimization doesn't replace meaning.

Now that we know the value of holding the horizon, it's time to reflect on what it truly means to keep leadership human-centered amid relentless acceleration. Let's bring all of this together and ensure our compass remains pointed at what matters most.

Generalists Were Built for This Moment

Not to be the fastest, or the flashiest.

But to be the ones who see across systems, hold competing truths, ask better questions, and lead people—not just processes—through the fog.

You don't have to outthink the machine on its terms.

You have to lead on yours.

Slow down when others rush.

Connect when others fragment.

Sense the ripple when others chase the trend.

Leadership isn't about mastering every change.

It's about staying anchored to what doesn't change:

Judgment. Integrity. Vision. Courage. Humanity.

The future isn't a machine problem.

It's a human one.

And that's why it still needs a human perspective.

Appendices

Appendix A

The Generalist's Advantage Toolkit for Leading in the Age of AI

These tools are designed to help you lead human-centered systems through complexity and acceleration. Use them to stay grounded, steer with discernment, and anchor your leadership in human judgment.

Five Ethical Checks Before Acting on AI Recommendations

Before accepting a machine-driven suggestion, slow down and ask:

Who is impacted beyond the immediate numbers?

Not just customers and shareholders—your people, your reputation, your future relationships.

What long-term trust or reputation could be affected?

Efficiency gains today can quietly erode what makes your organization credible.

What critical risks might the system not account for?

Machines are trained on patterns—not on consequences they can't predict.

Does this decision align with our values—or just our metrics?

If it's smart but not right, it's still wrong.

Would I be willing to explain this decision directly to those it affects?

If not, you're not ready to make it.

Five Conductor Cues for Leading AI-Human Systems

Watch for these moments where leadership—not speed—matters most:

When the technology outpaces the team's understanding:

Pause. Realign expectations. Never sacrifice clarity for velocity.

When specialists retreat into silos:

Rebuild bridges. Cross-pollinate perspectives early and often.

When data looks clean but tension rises:

Trust your gut. Human signals matter more than dashboard reports.

When speed starts replacing sense:

Slow the tempo. Leadership means protecting coherence, not just momentum.

When wins feel hollow:

Re-anchor the team to the real mission. Remind them what the work is for—not just what it accomplishes.

Five Horizon-Holding Questions for Long-View Leadership

Before every major move, ask yourself: What future impact am I responsible for beyond this decision?

Are we reinforcing the right habits—or just reacting to the immediate win?

Who will inherit the culture we're shaping right now?

What unintended consequences could ripple out five years from today?

Does this move align with the future story we want to tell?

Final Reminder

The system may move fast.

The tools may optimize.

But the future is still human-built.

Stay human.

Lead fully.

Hold the horizon.

Appendix B

Leadership Reflection Prompts for Generalists Leading in the Age of AI

Leading through complexity isn't just about making decisions faster.

It's about asking sharper questions before you move.

Use these prompts to think through your choices, sense the system you're working inside, and hold the human horizon —especially when the noise is pushing you to sprint.

You can use these for:

- Personal leadership reflection.
- Team discussions.
- Strategic planning sessions.
- Executive check-ins.

Thinking Across Systems

What ripple effects could this decision cause that aren't immediately obvious?

Who isn't in the room but should be influencing this conversation?

Where could silos or speed create blind spots?

What part of the system will resist this change even if the logic is sound?

Holding Ethics and Consequence

Does this move align with who we say we are—not just what we say we want?

If this plays out exactly as designed, what unintended harm might we create?

Would I be proud to stand in front of the people impacted and explain this decision?

Are we choosing speed because it's better—or because it's easier?

Leading Through AI Acceleration

What work are we handing over to machines—and what leadership work are we quietly abandoning?

How do we stay responsible for outcomes even when AI handles the process?

Where do we need human judgment to stay in the loop—not just human approval at the end?

Holding the Horizon

Are we making decisions that serve this quarter—or decisions that serve the mission?

Five years from now, will this move still feel right—or will it feel like a shortcut we regret?

What future are we building, one decision at a time—and are we proud of it?

Final Reminder

Leadership isn't just about navigating change.
It's about deciding who we become while we do it.

Slow down.
Ask better questions.
Hold the horizon.

Appendix C

Quick Index of Key Tools and Ideas

This index pulls together the leadership moves, frameworks, and reflection questions introduced throughout the book— so you can find what you need when you need it.

Use this as a quick map when you're navigating complexity and need a fast leadership anchor.

Leadership Shifts Introduced
- Lead the human system around the technology. (Chapter 1)
- Think across the system, not just inside silos. (Chapter 2)
- Conduct AI-human systems with rhythm, trust, and judgment. (Chapter 9)
- Hold the horizon steady when others sprint. (Chapter 10)

Key Tools and Frameworks
- Five Ethical Checks Before Acting on AI Recommendations (Chapter 8)
- Five Conductor Cues for Leading AI-Human Systems (Chapter 9)
- Five Horizon-Holding Leadership Questions (Chapter 10)
- Evaluating AI Tools: A Leadership Checklist (Appendix E)

Reflection Prompts Summary
- Scan for second- and third-order consequences before finalizing decisions.
- Sense who's missing from the decision room early.
- Question whether speed is helping or hurting c ore strategy.
- Anchor to long-term trust, not just immediate wins.
- Protect leadership responsibility, even in an AI-accelerated workflow.

The faster the world moves, the more valuable it is to have clear leadership anchors.

Use this book.
Use these tools.
But most of all—use your judgment.

That's what holds the horizon.

Appendix D

Working Smarter with AI:
A Human Leadership Guide

This isn't about learning how to prompt better. It's about thinking better—so you can lead beyond the prompt.

AI can assist. But leadership requires discernment, framing, and foresight. Use this guide not just to streamline tasks, but to deepen the way you think, decide, and communicate.

It's the fastest, dumbest worker you'll ever hire.

AI can be an incredible amplifier—but only if you lead it. Treat it like a powerful assistant, not a replacement for your judgment. This guide offers a human-centered approach to working with AI thoughtfully, practically, and responsibly.

Important Note:

This guide focuses on personal and leadership-driven use of AI—not enterprise-wide system building or technical model development.

You don't have to architect AI systems to lead wisely through them. You simply need to work thoughtfully with the tools now available, keeping your leadership, judgment, and humanity fully engaged.

Mindset: Lead the Machine, Don't Follow It

Everyday Smart Uses for AI

- Drafting: Use AI to create first-draft memos, summaries, proposals, and brainstorming outlines.

- Summarization: Summarize complex articles, research papers, or meeting notes quickly.

- Scenario Planning: Generate multiple potential outcomes to stress-test strategic decisions.

- Option Exploration: Use AI to surface non-obvious options without outsourcing final decisions.

- Internal Risk Scanning: Identify possible second-order effects or blind spots in a plan.

Framing Smarter Prompts: Leadership-Driven Questions

Good prompts don't happen by accident. Lead the machine by setting the right frame:

- **Set the Role:** "Act as [strategic advisor, cultural analyst, leadership coach]."

- **Frame the Scenario:** "You are advising a [type of organization] facing [challenge/context]."

- **Define the Goal:** "Suggest solutions that prioritize [values: trust, innovation, resilience, humanity]."

- **Request Depth:** "Include risks, trade-offs, second-order effects, and leadership considerations."

- **Ask for Multiple Perspectives:** "Offer at least two different strategic options if applicable."

Example: Bad Prompt vs. Good Prompt

Bad Prompt:

```
Give me a business strategy for next year.
```

Good Prompt:

```
Act as a brand strategist. Identify
three marketing initiatives for a
mid-sized services firm entering AI
markets. Prioritize initiatives that
build long-term customer trust and
human loyalty over short-term efficiency.
Include potential risks and long-term
brand impacts.
```

Designing Smarter AI Prompts: Five Steps

- Set the Role: "Act as [advisor, strategist, cultural analyst, leadership coach]..."

- Frame the Scenario: "You are advising a [industry/ size/context] organization facing [specific challenge]..."

- Define the Goal: "Suggest solutions that prioritize [values: trust, innovation, human leadership, etc.]..."

- Request Depth, Not Surface: "Include risks, trade-offs, second-order effects, and leadership implications."

- Ask for Multiple Perspectives: "Offer at least two different strategic options if applicable."

Leadership Reminders for AI Use

- Use the machine. Keep the mind.
- Technology accelerates decisions, but judgment must slow them enough to stay responsible.
- Curiosity is your ally. Fear is not.
- Leadership isn't about chasing faster answers. It's about anchoring better questions.

AI can amplify your work, but it will never replace the part of leadership that carries consequences, balances tensions, protects humanity, and holds the horizon.

Use the machine wisely.
Lead the system boldly.

Appendix E

Navigating AI Tools: A Starting Map
Evaluating AI Tools:
A Leadership Checklist

When considering new AI systems, leaders should look beyond speed and efficiency.

- Ask: Does this tool align with human-centered values?

- What unintended consequences could ripple from adopting it?

- How transparent is the tool's decision-making process?

- Does it enhance judgment or replace it?

- How will it shift trust, loyalty, or resilience inside the team?

New tools will keep coming. Your leadership judgment is what determines how wisely you use them.

The landscape of AI tools changes faster than any book could keep up with. New tools are launching, evolving, merging, or disappearing every month. What's listed here is a snapshot—not a full catalog and not a guarantee. The real skill isn't memorizing every new tool. It's learning how to work with them critically, creatively, and responsibly.

Stay curious. Stay discerning.
The tools will change. The leadership standards shouldn't.

Where to Find Updated AI Tool Lists:

Go to your favorite AI tool—ChatGPT, Perplexity, Grok, or any other—and type:

"Give me a list of current AI tools available to me for the purpose of _____."

Fill in the blank with whatever you're about to do—art, writing, research, business, anything.

You'll get an answer.

Snapshot of Common AI Tools (as of June 2025)

Writing and Content Generation

- ChatGPT (OpenAI) — Writing assistance, idea generation, research support
- Claude (Anthropic) — Context-aware writing, summarization
- Jasper — Marketing and creative writing automation
- Copy.ai — Content generation for businesses and marketing

Image and Design Generation

- Midjourney — Artistic and conceptual image generation
- DALL·E 3 (OpenAI) — Image generation from text prompts
- Canva AI — AI-driven design suggestions and templates

Voice and Video Tools
- ElevenLabs — Voice cloning and speech synthesis
- Descript — AI-powered audio/video editing and transcription
- Runway Gen-2 — Text-to-video generation and media editing

Data and Analytics Tools
- Perplexity AI — AI-powered search and research assistant
- Wizeline — AI-driven business intelligence and dashboards
- Polymer Search — AI-automated database exploration

Productivity and Workflow Tools
- Notion AI — Writing, organizing, and note summarization
- Zapier AI — Automating workflows across apps and services
- Motion — AI calendar and task management

Research and Knowledge Discovery
- Elicit (by Ought) — Literature review and research synthesis
- Consensus — AI for scientific research summary and discovery

Code and Development Support
- GitHub Copilot — AI pair programming assistant
- Replit Ghostwriter — Coding support and automation

Specialized-Use Tools
- Beautiful.ai — AI-assisted slide and presentation creation
- Tome — AI-driven storytelling and pitch deck creation
- Otter.ai — AI meeting transcription and collaboration tool

Leadership Reminder

The tool is only as useful as the thinking behind it.

Always use your judgment. New doesn't always mean better.

Fast doesn't always mean wise.

New AI systems will keep getting faster.
But the leadership challenge stays the same:

- Stay human.
- Stay responsible.
- Stay clear about what matters.

Use the tools.
Lead the system.

The future still needs a human to make the right call.

Appendix F

Framing Better Questions for AI (and Leadership)

A strategic toolkit for prompting, interpreting, and leading well in the machine age.

Why Prompts Are a Leadership Tool

Prompts aren't just about getting better answers. They're about asking better questions—ones rooted in strategy, ethics, and impact.

In the age of AI, leadership lives beyond the prompt. These tools help you prompt with purpose, not just precision.

The prompts in this section are designed to help you use AI intelligently—without outsourcing leadership judgment. Use them to stretch thinking, surface blind spots, and challenge the easy answers.

Remember:

AI is only as sharp as the frame you give it.

Lead the question. Don't chase the output.

Five Steps to Designing Smarter Prompts

- Set the Role:
  "Act as [advisor, strategist, cultural analyst, leadership coach]…" (Assigns the AI a perspective.)

- Frame the Scenario:
  "You are advising a [industry/size/context] organization facing [specific challenge]…" (Anchors advice inside a real-world setting.)

- Define the Goal:
  "Suggest solutions that prioritize [values: trust, innovation, human leadership, etc.]…" (Clarifies the outcome you care about.)

- Request Depth, Not Surface:
  "Include risks, trade-offs, second-order effects, and leadership implications." (Forces complexity instead of easy answers.)

- Ask for Multiple Perspectives:
  "Offer at least two different strategic options if applicable." (Expands the system view.)

Example:

Bad Prompt:

```
Give me some ideas for marketing next year.
```

Good Prompt:

```
Act as a brand strategist. Identify three
marketing initiatives for a mid-size
services firm entering AI markets.
Prioritize initiatives that build long-
term customer trust and human loyalty
over short-term efficiency. Include
potential risks and long-term brand
impacts.
```

Strategic Prompts by Use Case

Strategy and Risk Scanning

- Strategic Disruption Awareness:
  "Act as a strategic advisor. Based on current AI-driven market shifts, identify three major external risks a mid-size company in [your industry] could face in the next three years. Include second-order effects."

- Long-Term Trust Risk:
  "What long-term brand risks could emerge from aggressive AI adoption in customer-facing functions? Focus on loss of human connection and perceived authenticity."

- Scenario Planning:
  "Outline two future scenarios for how AI could either strengthen or weaken mid-market firms by 2030. Include leadership challenges unique to each scenario."

Culture, Talent, and Internal Leadership

- Cultural Side Effects of AI Adoption:
  "Identify hidden cultural risks when automating 20% of internal workflows. What leadership strategies could preserve trust and morale?"

- Talent Strategy Reframe:
  "Suggest ways a generalist-skilled workforce could become a competitive advantage in a market increasingly dominated by AI-specialist hiring trends."

- Trust and Transparency Building:
  "Generate a communication plan outline for leaders introducing AI into workflows while maintaining transparency, respect, and employee agency."

Customer and Market Positioning

- Customer Sentiment Shift:
  "How might customer expectations shift if AI-driven service becomes the norm in our sector? Suggest three ways a human-centered brand could differentiate itself."

- Ethical Customer Engagement:
  "Propose best practices for using AI to enhance customer experience without crossing ethical lines regarding privacy, consent, or manipulation."

Innovation and Future Framing

- Future Sensing:
  "What emerging technologies (beyond AI) could reshape our industry's assumptions within the next 5–10 years? Focus on cross-disciplinary impact."

- Narrative Framing:
  "Suggest three ways leaders can frame the role of AI inside the company narrative to strengthen identity, purpose, and employee pride."

Appendix G

Leading Your Own GPT Initiative

You don't have to code a model.

You do have to lead it wisely.

As AI systems like GPT evolve, more companies are considering building or customizing their own models—training them on internal data, workflows, and priorities.

It sounds cutting-edge.

It can be.

But it's not just a technical project.

It's a leadership decision—with real stakes for trust, strategy, and culture.

If your organization considers building a proprietary GPT (or customizing an LLM), here's what leadership means:

- Define Human-Centered Guardrails First
    - What ethical standards must any AI-generated advice meet?
    - What redlines are non-negotiable, even if optimization suggests otherwise?
    - What human checks will remain in the loop?

- Prioritize Long-Term Trust Over Short-Term Efficiency
    - Models trained only on speed metrics will drive behavior you might regret.
    - Build trust into the system from the beginning—not after mistakes.

- Align the Model's Purpose with Strategic Purpose
    - What is this GPT designed to amplify?
    - Is it tuned for cost-cutting, customer loyalty, innovation, resilience?
    - Be intentional—or the system will optimize for whatever is easiest.

- Involve Cross-Disciplinary Voices Early
    - Don't let only tech teams set the parameters.
    - Legal, HR, brand, ethics, operations—all should shape the model.

- Own the Ongoing Stewardship
    - AI models aren't static.
    - As your system evolves, leadership must keep regrounding it in human judgment, ethics, and meaning.

Bottom Line:

You don't have to engineer the model.
But you do have to lead the system it shapes.
Customization doesn't remove your responsibility.
It deepens it.

The future isn't just about building faster tools.
It's about building better systems—and holding the horizon as we do.

Joe Curcillo

Explore The Generalist's Advantage Leadership Suite
The journey doesn't end here.

The Generalist's Advantage Leadership Suite is a connected body of work designed to help leaders think across systems, lead through complexity, and hold the human horizon steady through accelerating change. The suite includes:

The Generalist's Advantage: How to Harness the Raw Power of Cross-Disciplinary Thinking. This flagship book explores the joy of being a generalist and encourages you to break out of your own silos and improve all aspects of your life.

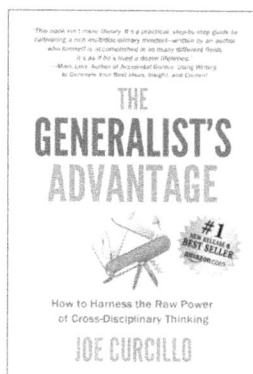

THE GENERALIST'S ADVANTAGE

#1 BEST SELLER

How to Harness the Raw Power of Cross-Disciplinary Thinking

JOE CURCILLO

Symphony of Disciplines: The Symphony of Disciplines Journal: An Intra-Personal Assessment Tool for Empowered Cross-Disciplinary Success. Your guide to unlocking multidimensional thinking for fully integrated leadership across disciplines, identities, and experiences.

Beyond the Prompt: Leading with Purpose in the Age of AI In a world racing toward automation, *Beyond the Prompt* offers leaders a clear, steady guide to navigating AI with judgment, humanity, and confidence.

Hold the Horizon: Lead from the Liminal into the Fog: The Generalist's Advantage™ Tactical Field Guide for Leading Across Silos, Systems, and Uncertainty
This is your tactical field guide for leading through silos, systems, and uncertainty—designed for the ones who see more, hold more, and lead when the path ahead is anything but clear.

Each book stands on its own.
Together, they form a living framework for human-centered leadership built for a complex world.

The future needs generalists.
It needs system-sense-makers.
It needs a human hand to guide us

Learn more at **www.TheGeneralistsAdvantage.com**

About the Author

Joe Curcillo: The Maestro of Integration and Cross-Disciplinary Thinking

Joe is the author of *The Generalist's Advantage: How to Harness the Raw Power of Cross-Disciplinary Thinking*. In a world that demands innovation and adaptability, Joe Curcillo has dedicated his life to transforming diverse skills into strategic solutions for leaders and organizations. With a career spanning law, engineering, entertainment, and business leadership, Joe has spent decades solving complex problems and inspiring innovation through cross-disciplinary thinking.

As a celebrated trial attorney, strategic advisor, and acclaimed speaker, Joe has empowered countless individuals and teams to turn chaos into clarity and thrive in high-pressure environments. His unique ability to bridge disciplines has earned him recognition as a thought leader in leadership development, creative problem-solving, and professional growth.

Joe is also a fine artist, magician, and storyteller who believes every skill—no matter how unrelated it seems—plays a critical role in crafting a meaningful life. This belief forms the foundation of his mission: helping leaders and organizations orchestrate their own symphonies of success.

He lives near Hershey, Pennsylvania, with his wife and an endless supply of caffeine, always ready to explore new intersections of creativity and strategy.

Joe continues to explore new intersections of creativity and strategy, sharing his insights through speaking, coaching, and his books. His work inspires leaders to embrace their multifaceted identities and thrive in an ever-changing world.